STATE V. COLE

Second Edition

STATE V. COLE

Second Edition

Michael S. Sands

Professor of Law and
Director of Trial Advocacy
University of the Pacific
McGeorge School of Law
(Retired)

NATIONAL INSTITUTE FOR TRIAL ADVOCACY

Reprint Permission

National Institute for Trial Advocacy
361 Centennial Parkway, Suite 220
Louisville, CO 80027

Phone: (800) 225-6482
Fax: (720) 890-7069
E-mail: permissions@nita.org

ISBN 978-1-60156-102-2

FBA 1102

11 10 09   10 9 8 7 6 5 4 3 2 1

Printed in the United States of America

ACKNOWLEDGMENTS

The contributions of several people deserve special attention. Gregory D. Reiber, MD, a board-certified anatomical, clinical, and forensic pathologist who served as an autopsy surgeon for the Sacramento County Coroner's Office greatly assisted the author in preparing the autopsy report and accompanying diagrams.

Prof. Joseph E. Taylor, Director of Trial Advocacy at McGeorge School of Law, University of the Pacific, provided many invaluable suggestions and greatly assisted in editing the case for publication, as did Michael Rothschild of Rothschild, Wishek & Sands, Sacramento, California.

CONTENTS

INTRODUCTION

This is a homicide case. The State of Nita has alleged that the defendant, Walter "Wally" Cole shot and killed Donald Abbott. Cole previously had an affair with Abbott's wife, Virginia "Ginny" Abbott.

The defendant was arrested on July 24, YR-1, by Inspector Jamie Stanton of the Darrow County Sheriff's Office. A preliminary hearing was held October 16–18, YR-1, and the defendant was held to answer on an open charge of murder. An information was thereafter filed in the District Court on November 2, YR-1, charging Cole with Murder in the First Degree, a violation of Section 101 of the Nita Criminal Code.

The applicable law is contained in the memo, and proposed jury instructions are set forth at the end of the file.

All years in these materials are stated in the following form:

YR-0 indicates the actual year in which the case is being tried (i.e., the present year);

YR-1 indicates the next preceding year (please use the actual year);

YR-2 indicates the second preceding year (please use the actual year), etc.

SPECIAL INSTRUCTIONS FOR USE AS A FULL TRIAL

When this case file is used for a full trial, the following witnesses may be called by the parties:

State of Nita:	Virginia Abbott
	Leslie LoMonico, MD
	Jan Newman
	Jamie Stanton
	Pat Miller
Defendant:	Walter Cole
	Brenda Cole
	Terry Lee
	Dale Baxter, MD

LIMITATION ON WITNESSES

Each party is limited to four witnesses.

REQUIRED STIPULATIONS

1. Because the prosecution may call no more than four witnesses, the testimony of either Dr. Leslie LoMonico or Jan Newman may be presented by the transcript of the preliminary hearing, or by a videotape of a conditional examination, if it is available. If the prosecution fails to produce any evidence from either of these witnesses, then the defense may present that evidence by the transcript or the videotape. The prosecution may call both Dr. LoMonico and Jan Newman and eliminate another witness.

2. If the prosecution does not call Virginia Abbott as a witness, the defense may move to admit her preliminary hearing testimony under any applicable authority.

3. The preliminary hearing was transcribed by a certified shorthand reporter. The transcript of the preliminary hearing accurately states the testimony as given at the preliminary hearing.

4. If the rules of court for this trial preclude rebuttal witnesses, a witness may be asked what another potential witness said on an earlier occasion as a possible prior inconsistent statement. If the second witness has not yet testified, a hearsay objection will be overruled subject to a motion to strike, if the second witness does not testify or testifies consistent with the statement to the first witness.

PRETRIAL MOTIONS

The defendant moved to dismiss the information on the grounds that the evidence presented at the preliminary hearing was legally insufficient to support the holding order. The defendant also moved to suppress his entire statement to Deputy Miller, alleging a violation of *Miranda v. Arizona*. The court denied both motions. These issues may not be relitigated at trial.

For tactical purposes, the prosecution may request a conviction for an offense less than first-degree murder. If this is done, the jury instructions and verdict form should be modified accordingly.

IN THE DISTRICT COURT
OF THE STATE OF NITA
COUNTY OF DARROW

THE STATE OF NITA	)	
vs.	)	Case No. CR 55827
WALTER COLE,	)	INFORMATION
Defendant.	)	

THE STATE OF NITA does hereby charge the defendant, WALTER COLE with the following offense under the Criminal Code of the State of Nita:

That on the 24th day of July, YR-1, at and within the County of Darrow, Walter Cole committed the crime of Murder in the First Degree, a violation of Section 101 of the Criminal Code of the State of Nita, in that he knowingly, willfully, deliberately, and with the intent to cause the death of Donald Abbott, caused the death of Donald Abbott, a human being, contrary to the form, force, and effect of the law of the State of Nita and against the peace and dignity of the People of the State of Nita.

DATED: November 1, YR-1

J. E. Taylor

_____

J. E. Taylor
District Attorney

Darrow County
State of Nita

DARROW COUNTY SHERIFF'S OFFICE
OFFENSE REPORT

VICTIM:	Donald Abbott	**CASE NO. YR-1-7532**
	DOB: 03/20/YR-38	
	Sex: Male	
SUSPECT:	Walter Cole	
	DOB: 10/05/YR-41	
	Sex: Male	
LOCATION:	Glenwood Canyon Road, Highlands Vista, approx. 0.3 mile north of Camptown Road (at entrance to Community Church).	
OFFENSE:	Possible murder (NCC 101)	
DATE OF REPORT:	July 25, YR-1	
OFFICER:	Pat Miller, #170	

While on routine patrol on Highlands Vista Road, I received a call from dispatch at 1955 hours on July 24, YR-1, informing me of a possible shooting on Glenwood Canyon Road north of Camptown Road. I responded Code 3. As I turned north on Glenwood Canyon Road I saw the rescue squad proceeding north in front of me. They disappeared over the hill to the north of Camptown Road. As I proceeded down the hill toward the Community Church I saw the rescue squad van parked on the right side of the road. I pulled in behind it at 2002 hours.

Off to the right was a driveway into the church parking lot. The driveway is also shared by one private residence, which I later learned belonged to the suspect, Walter Cole. Lying on his back in the driveway, his head in a general northerly direction, was the victim, a man later learned to be Donald Abbott. The suspect, Walter Cole, was being led by an EMT toward a black and silver Chevy Blazer parked in the driveway behind a Toyota pickup truck. The Blazer had an empty trailer attached to it. The driver's door was open, and the window in that door was down. Two EMTs were providing CPR to Mr. Abbott.

I walked over to where Mr. Abbott was lying in the driveway. He appeared to have been shot at least once in the chest. One of the EMTs told me they could not find any vital signs. They told me that an ambulance would be there momentarily, so I ordered them to have Mr. Abbott taken to Nita Community Hospital, which was the closest hospital with an emergency room.

At 2006 Officers Warren and Padilla arrived. I informed them of what I knew and asked them to secure the scene. At 2007 the ambulance arrived, and Mr. Abbott was taken from the scene.

At 2009 I approached the man standing by the Blazer with one of the EMTs. I asked for identification, and he gave me a valid Nita driver's license identifying him as Walter Cole of 20717 Glenwood Canyon Road, Highlands Vista. This address was located behind the Community Church and shared the driveway where we were standing.

I asked Mr. Cole if he knew who had shot the victim, and he said that he had. I asked him if he was still armed, and he said that he wasn't, that the gun was still in his Blazer. I looked through the open driver's door and saw a .38 caliber revolver sticking up between the driver's seat and the console. I left the gun where it was until I could photograph it, and I moved Mr. Cole over to my patrol car. I then advised Mr. Cole of his constitutional rights per *Miranda*, and he stated that he understood them and would waive them. He indicated that he wanted to tell me what happened.

STATEMENT OF WALTER COLE

Mr. Cole said that the man who was shot was Donald Abbott, the husband of Ginny Abbott, a woman with whom he had an affair for about three years. The affair ended around the first of this year.

Mr. Cole said that he is married to Brenda Cole, and he thought she was in the house across the street because he had sent her there to call for help. He and Brenda have three minor children. He also said the Abbotts have four minor children, and he kept asking how Mr. Abbott was. I continually told him that I didn't know, that Mr. Abbott had been taken to the hospital, and that I would let him know when I learned Abbott's condition. Mr. Cole said that he worked at the Nita Community Hospital, knew that they had a good emergency room, and that he hoped Abbott would live.

Mr. Cole said that Brenda had learned of the affair after it had ended in January. She called Ginny about the affair, and as a result Abbott also learned of the affair. Ever since, Abbott has been trying to harm Cole. On one occasion in January, when Cole was parked near the school on Glenwood Canyon Road, Abbott came up to the Blazer and began banging on the window and hollering that he would kill Cole. Fortunately, the windows were up and the door locked, and Cole drove off. On another occasion, Abbott chased Cole all over Apple Valley before Cole finally got away. Just several weeks ago, in late May or early June, Abbott came up behind Cole while on Glenwood Canyon Road and chased Cole all the way to Cole's home. Shortly after that, Abbott got in front of Cole on Glenwood Canyon and led him home, trying to get Cole to stop, but Cole wouldn't stop.

Tonight, Cole and his wife had driven into Nita City to take their all-terrain vehicle to a repair shop. After getting dinner, they were on their way home, pulling the empty trailer. On Glenwood Canyon they were going a little less than the posted limit of 45 mph when Cole suddenly heard a loud noise to his left. He saw Abbott passing at a high rate of speed. Abbott cut in front of Cole and slammed on his brakes, almost coming to a complete stop. Abbott kept motioning with his hand for Cole to pull over, but Cole wouldn't stop, so they continued up the road at between two and five miles per hour. Just as they passed the fire station Abbott suddenly sped up and disappeared over the hill. During this whole time Brenda was screaming things like, "Oh God," "He's going to kill us," and "Let me out."

As they came over the hill, Cole braked to turn into his driveway. The road curves to the right, and Cole could not see Abbott. As Cole turned into the driveway, he suddenly saw Abbott's truck parked across the driveway so that Cole could not pass. Cole slammed on his brakes and brought his car to a stop about ten feet from the pickup. He thought about backing up, but with the trailer he couldn't do it quickly. He saw Abbott rushing around the left rear side of the pickup. Abbott was moving rapidly and seemed to be saying something, but Cole couldn't hear because Brenda was still yelling. Abbott came up to the driver's door of Cole's car and reached through the open window with his head and both arms, reaching for Cole. At this time Abbott said, "Your time is now." Cole leaned towards Brenda and twisted so that he was facing Abbott. Suddenly, as Cole tells it, the gun went off. Abbott immediately staggered back, turned slowly to his left, and fell face forward on the ground. Cole told his wife to go across the street and call for help. Cole went over to Abbott and found a carotid pulse. He turned Abbott over, opened his shirt, and began CPR. Approximately thirty seconds before the emergency squad arrived he no longer could find a pulse.

Cole has owned the gun for many years. Previously it was kept unloaded in the house and was used only when Cole and his family went four-wheeling. Primarily, it was protection against rattlesnakes. However, after

Abbott told Cole in January that he (Abbott) wanted to kill Cole, Cole loaded the gun and kept it under the driver's seat. He never tried to use it on any of the other occasions when Abbott chased him. On this evening, he does not remember taking it out from under the seat and does not remember pulling the trigger, although he knows he did.

After taking the statement from Cole, I allowed him to use a hose in the yard across the street to wash the blood off his hands and arms. I then returned him to my patrol car. Before I could put him in the car, a woman walked up to talk to him. Cole said, "It's all over, babe." I stepped between them and asked if she was Mrs. Cole. Cole responded that she was Mrs. Abbott, and introduced her as "Ginny." I informed Mrs. Abbott that her husband had been taken to Nita Community Hospital and that perhaps she should go there. I asked her to remain there until an officer could talk to her. I then seated Cole in the rear of my patrol car.

I then obtained a camera from the trunk of my car and took many photographs of the scene, including the vehicles and the gun inside the Blazer. I then removed the gun from the car. Inspection revealed that it was a Smith & Wesson .38 caliber police special, serial number 5K85357. It was fully loaded except for one expended cartridge under the hammer. The gun was taken into evidence.

Inspector Stanton, who was now on the scene and in charge of the investigation, instructed me to take Cole to the hospital to have a blood sample drawn, and then take him to our office in Nita City. I arrived at the hospital at 2200 hours and arranged for a nurse, Marilyn Paulson, to draw a blood sample from Cole. The sample was drawn at 2206. The sealed vial of blood was given to me for booking into evidence. While at the hospital I learned that Mr. Abbott had died, so I took Cole to the Darrow County Jail and booked him for murder.

DARROW COUNTY SHERIFF'S OFFICE
OFFENSE REPORT

VICTIM:	Donald Abbott	**CASE NO. YR-1-7532**
	DOB: 03/20/YR-38	
	Sex: Male	
SUSPECT:	Walter Cole	
	DOB: 10/05/YR-41	
	Sex: Male	
LOCATION:	Glenwood Canyon Rd. at Community Church	
OFFENSE:	Murder	
DATE OF REPORT:	July 26, YR-1	
OFFICER:	Inspector Jamie Stanton, #32	

On July 24, YR-1, I was attending a community meeting in the Apple Valley area of Darrow County. At approximately 2005 I received a message on my pager to call dispatch. Doing so, I learned that there had been a shooting in Highlands Vista at the Community Church. I was asked to take charge of the investigation, so I left immediately for the scene, arriving at 2020 hours. I was informed that the victim, Donald Abbott, had been taken by ambulance to Nita Community Hospital and might not survive. Sergeant Kapandritis and Deputy Padilla had secured the scene to preserve all evidence. Deputy Warren introduced me to Terry Lee, who had been parked across the street watching the officers. I took a statement from Lee.

STATEMENT OF TERRY LEE

Lee is an insurance agent in Nita City. On this evening, Lee was delivering a policy to the home of a client on Glenwood Canyon Road. At approximately 1940 hours Lee was driving northbound on Glenwood Canyon, followed by a young woman in a red Mustang convertible. Lee believes this woman, who is unknown, may have seen even more than Lee.

Approaching the trailer park, Lee caught up to a Blazer pulling an empty trailer. The Blazer was going less than the speed limit of 45 mph. Because of the curves in the road and the oncoming traffic, Lee could not pass. Just before reaching Highlands Vista Road Lee heard a loud noise and saw a Toyota pickup truck pass the Mustang, Lee, and then the Blazer, staying on the wrong side of the road even around the curves. When the pickup got in front of the Blazer, the pickup suddenly braked and slowed to about 5 mph. The Blazer blocked Lee's view of the pickup. They all continued at about 5 mph until they reached the fire station, when the pickup drove off and disappeared over the hill. As Lee crested the hill, the Blazer was braking and signaling a right turn, so Lee also slowed. The Blazer turned into the church's driveway. As Lee passed the driveway, the pickup could be seen blocking the driveway. A man appeared to be walking around the rear left side of the pickup toward the Blazer. As Lee drove on, a sound like a backfire was heard, but Lee paid no attention.

After dropping off the policy about one-fourth of a mile down the road, Lee headed back to the interstate. When passing the church, Lee saw one man lying on the ground and another man kneeling over him. It

NATIONAL INSTITUTE FOR TRIAL ADVOCACY

appeared that someone was hurt, so Lee called 911 on his cell phone and was told that help was already on the way. Lee pulled over to wait. Within a few minutes the rescue squad arrived with three EMTs, followed very closely by a sheriff's unit. Lee waited until other deputies arrived and then contacted them.

Lee lives at 1372 Brubeck Court in Nita City. Lee's phone number is 735-7002, and he will be available at any time for additional investigation.

After taking Lee's statement, I learned that Mrs. Cole was supposed to be in the house across the street from the church. I went across the street to 20720 Glenwood Canyon Road and spoke to the owner, Fern Grable. She told me that Mrs. Cole was inside. She told me that Mrs. Cole had come running over about eight o'clock, yelling for her to call the police because her husband had shot someone. Mrs. Grable is about eighty years old and admitted to being a little hard of hearing. She said that she had not heard any shots.

I found Mrs. Cole in Mrs. Grable's house. Mrs. Cole asked me the condition of Mr. Abbott, and I told her that I didn't know, that he had been taken to Nita Community Hospital. Mrs. Cole was visibly upset but appeared to be reasonably calm and composed. She agreed to give me a statement at this time.

STATEMENT OF BRENDA COLE

Mrs. Cole said that she has been married to Walter Cole, who is known as Wally, for sixteen years. It is her second marriage and his first. They have three children, ages fifteen, thirteen, and eleven. Her husband is the supervising radiology technician at Nita Community Hospital. They live across the street in the house behind the church. They share the driveway with the church.

The man who was shot, Don Abbott, is the husband of Ginny Abbott, the woman with whom her husband was having an affair. In January of this year, Brenda learned of the affair, which had allegedly ended just before she learned of it. Brenda was so angry that she called Ginny right away, about eight o'clock in the morning. Apparently, Don was still home, and he learned of the affair. A few nights later when Wally came home, he said that Don had found him parked near the school and had pounded on the car and threatened to kill him. Abbott had then chased Wally all around Apple Valley. Wally was so scared that instead of coming directly home he first went to the hospital to be sure that Abbott wouldn't come to the house.

A week or so later, Brenda was working in the kitchen when she heard Wally's Blazer driving very fast up the driveway. She looked out the window and saw a pickup truck, looking just like the one she saw tonight, drive halfway up the driveway, then stop and back down. Wally told her that Don had caught up with him on Glenwood Canyon and chased him all the way home.

This was the only time before tonight that she had ever seen Don Abbott or his pickup. She understands that he is a long-distance truck driver and is often out of town, which is apparently how Mrs. Abbott had so much time for the affair. Tonight, she and Mr. Cole had driven into town to take their ATV for repair. On the way home, they stopped for dinner and to get some ice cream for the kids. As they were driving on Glenwood Canyon Road, Abbott passed them and then slowed almost to a stop. She was terrified. After a while Abbott sped off, but when they turned into their driveway, Abbott had parked his truck blocking the way to their home.

Mrs. Cole remembers Abbott coming around the rear of his truck toward them. She was screaming in fear and doesn't remember much, but she heard Wally's gun fire once, and then he told her to call for help. She never saw Wally get the gun and doesn't know where he got it.

I asked permission to detach the trailer so that I could impound the Blazer. She gave permission but asked for the ice cream. I retrieved an insulated bag with a quart of ice cream from the rear seat and gave it to her. I then allowed Mrs. Cole to return home; she was not allowed to talk with Mr. Cole at this time.

We detached the trailer from the Blazer, and I ordered the Blazer to be impounded at the DCSO yard.

After leaving Sergeant Kapandritis in charge of completing the collection of evidence, I then went to Nita Community Hospital, arriving just after 2200 hours. Deputy Miller informed me that Abbott had been declared dead on arrival at the hospital. Deputy Miller also introduced me to Virginia Abbott.

Mrs. Abbott was being consoled by a friend, who apparently had driven her to the hospital. I expressed my condolences to Mrs. Abbott and told her it was important to gather information about the killing as quickly as possible. She agreed to talk with me at this time. The hospital allowed me to use one of the offices so that we could talk privately.

STATEMENT OF VIRGINIA ABBOTT

Mrs. Abbott was born on June 7, YR-37. Her husband was born March 20, YR-38. They had been married for fifteen years and have four children, aged eight through thirteen. The first ten years of the marriage were difficult. Donald Abbott drank heavily, and when he did he became violent and abusive, especially to her. They were living in Idaho at the time, and she often called the police. They would order her husband to leave the home, but they never arrested him, so there probably isn't any record. He does have a record, however, because about ten years ago he was caught with a substantial amount of cocaine. He pleaded guilty and was put on probation because it was his first offense.

About six years ago, Mr. Abbott went through counseling and stopped using drugs and abusing alcohol. He obtained a new driving position with Nita Express, and they moved to Highlands Vista. They live at 3535 Grandview Drive, just off Highlands Vista Road. Don kept his truck—not the pickup—at the yard in North Nita, about fifteen minutes down the interstate from Glenwood Canyon Road. Mrs. Abbott keeps one gun in the house. It is a .22 caliber revolver. She wanted it because Don was gone so much of the time. It is kept loaded and locked in her bedroom. Mr. Abbott knew where the key was, but she doesn't think any of the kids do. Mr. Abbott also kept a handgun in his truck, also for protection. Sometimes he brought it home between trips, but she hadn't seen it on this trip, so she assumes it is still in the truck.

After moving to Nita, Mr. Abbott replaced abuse with indifference. He was usually gone from home for long stretches at a time, and when he was home, all he did was play with the kids or watch television. They never did anything together. After settling into their new home, she obtained employment at Nita Community Hospital in the admissions office. It was here that she met Wally. He was very nice and soft spoken and never drank alcohol. At first it was just a casual, kidding-type relationship, but about three years ago they began an affair. It continued until the first of this year. It was ended mutually, and they still continue to talk to each other regularly.

One day in January, just after the affair had ended, she received a phone call from Brenda Cole about eight o'clock in the morning. Don was home that day. Brenda was screaming at her about being a home wrecker. Don couldn't help but hear. He became upset, but they talked about it and decided to try to keep the marriage together for the sake of the kids.

A couple of nights later, Don came in and said that he had caught Wally down by the school and had chased him all over Apple Valley. He said that if he could have caught him, he would have killed him. She tried to get him to calm down, but he was so upset. She knows of at least three other times when Don tried to find Wally. On at least one of these times Wally wasn't even aware of it at the time, but she told him later. Don and she were in Nita, and Don saw Wally driving the other way. Don tried to make a U-turn but was tied up in the heavy traffic. Wally just drove away, oblivious to the whole thing. Don was again threatening to kill Wally. She and Wally have spoken about once or twice a month since January, and she told him all about it. She also told him to be careful because she was never sure where Don had his gun when he came home.

Today, Don came home from one trip and was going to start another. He left the truck in the Nita Express yard in North Nita at about 4:00 p.m. and drove home in the pickup. He was supposed to pick up the truck again about 8:00 p.m. At home, he showered, had dinner, and talked with the kids about their activities. Her car needs repairs, so she was going to drive him back to the truck and then use his pickup while he was traveling. They left the house about 7:20 p.m., went down Highlands Vista Road, and then Glenwood Canyon Road to the interstate. As they were on the on-ramp, Don saw Wally and Brenda on the off-ramp on the other side of the interstate. They were in Wally's Blazer and were pulling their flatbed trailer. Don immediately slammed on the brakes and said, "I'm going to kill that son-of-a-bitch." She told Don to calm down and reminded him that he had to take the truck out at 8:00 p.m. Don continued driving down the interstate for about a half mile or so, and then he slammed on the brakes again and said, "I'll get that son-of-a-bitch if it's the last thing I do." He then made a U-turn over the center median and sped back up the interstate.

When they got to the top of the Glenwood Canyon off-ramp she told Don to let her out. She truly was afraid to see what was going to happen. She also thought that if she slowed Don down by getting out, perhaps Wally would have time to get home before Don caught him. When she got out she waited by the Park-and-Ride for Don to come back. A short time later she heard a siren and saw a Sheriff's car come off the interstate and speed up Glenwood Canyon Road. Almost immediately after that she saw an ambulance come speeding by. She was afraid that Don had been in a wreck. She ran down the street until she came to the home of a friend, Jeanne West. She told Jeanne what had happened and asked for a ride. They drove down Glenwood Canyon Road but never found an accident. When she got to Wally's house, she saw his Blazer. At first, she didn't even see Don's truck. She got out and ran over to Wally to ask what had happened. He said something like, "It's all over." Then an officer told her Don had been shot and had been taken to this hospital, so she had Jeanne drive her here.

She never saw a gun or any weapon in Don's pickup tonight. Since he was going back on the road tonight, she assumed that he had left his gun in the truck.

She doesn't know what she will do now. She doesn't want to stay here, but she will until this case is finished. Then she will probably move to Oregon to be near her parents.

After taking the statement from Mrs. Abbott, I asked her to accompany me while I looked for her husband's gun. We first drove to the Nita Express yard in North Nita. Using a set of keys that had been taken from Mr. Abbott's body, I opened Abbott's truck with Mrs. Abbott's permission. In the glove box I found a .357 Smith & Wesson revolver. It was fully loaded with no expended shells. It was quite dusty and looked as if it had not been fired for some time. Since the gun obviously did not play any role in the killing, I unloaded it and then returned it to Mrs. Abbott.

We next drove up the interstate to Glenwood Canyon Road. After getting off we crossed the interstate and then got on the on-ramp. I drove slowly until Mrs. Abbott told me to stop where her husband had stopped when he saw Mr. and Mrs. Cole. This spot was approximately 0.15 mile from the top of the on-ramp. I then continued down the interstate until Mrs. Abbott showed me where her husband had stopped a second time and made the U-turn. This was approximately 0.6 mile from the end of the on-ramp. There had been a serious accident at this location earlier in the week, and there were so many marks in the median area I could not find any that I could definitely attribute to Mr. Abbott's U-turn. I then made a U-turn myself and went back to the scene of the shooting.

The CSI officers had completed their investigation. The Blazer had already been towed to our yard, but the trailer and the pickup were still there. I searched the vehicle carefully for weapons, including in the toolbox in the bed of the pickup, but I found no gun of any type. I then released the pickup to Mrs. Abbott.

STATEMENT OF DALE BAXTER, MD

On July 25, YR-1, at 1330 hours, I returned to Nita Community Hospital and spoke to Dr. Dale Baxter, Walter Cole's immediate supervisor. Dr. Baxter said that Cole was considered to be an excellent worker. He supervised the other technicians in the radiology department with a firm but friendly hand and was well-liked by everyone. Even though Cole had seniority, he often volunteered to work on holidays so the others could be off, and he never complained about having to come in during his time off for an emergency.

One night last January, Dr. Baxter was on duty at the hospital while Cole was off. Cole unexpectedly came into the hospital. He looked upset and scared and was "white as a ghost." The doctor asked Cole what was the matter, and Cole replied that a man had been chasing him all over Apple Valley trying to kill him and that he was afraid to go home for fear the man would follow him. The doctor asked why the man was trying to hurt him, and Cole said that he didn't want to discuss that now, he just wanted the doctor to go outside and see if a black Toyota pickup truck was anywhere to be seen. The doctor went outside but could not see any such vehicle, so Cole then left, presumably to go home. As he left Cole said, "If it's trouble he wants, it's trouble he'll get."

Dr. Baxter indicated concern with Cole's situation and stated that as long as Cole was available to work he would be allowed to do so.

AUTOPSY OF DONALD ABBOTT

At 1500 hours I reported to the coroner's office to observe the autopsy of Donald Abbott by Dr. Leslie LoMonico. During the autopsy, all of Abbott's clothing was given to me to be booked into evidence. Dr. LoMonico removed a metal projectile from Abbott's body. It appeared to be a badly damaged .38 slug, which I also took into evidence. At the end of the autopsy Dr. LoMonico said it was obvious that death had been caused by a single gunshot wound. (See Dr. LoMonico's autopsy report for details.)

MEETING WITH CRIMINALIST

At 1700 hours I met with Jan Newman, a criminalist from the Nita Department of Justice. Newman informed me that an inspection of the Blazer showed traces of gunpowder at the upper and lower edges of the window opening in the driver's door. A couple of latent fingerprints had been located on the outside of the door. I asked Newman to compare the latents with both Abbott's and Cole's fingerprints. I also turned over Abbott's clothing and the slug recovered from Abbott's body to Newman. I asked that the clothing be checked for gunpowder residue and that the slug be compared with a slug fired from Cole's gun. Newman promised a complete report as soon as possible. (See Newman's report for details.)

MEETING WITH DISTRICT ATTORNEY

At 1800 hours I met with District Attorney J. E. Taylor and his chief investigator, T. J. Leach. We reviewed all of the evidence known at that time. In light of the fact that Abbott was totally unarmed and there was a car door between Cole and Abbott, it was felt that the shooting of Abbott was excessive force for the circumstances and that Cole should be charged with the murder of Abbott.

STATE OF NITA, COUNTY OF DARROW
OFFICE OF THE CORONER
AUTOPSY REPORT

Name: ABBOTT, DONALD **Age:** 37 **Sex:** M **Case No.:** YR-1-134 **DCSO No.:** YR-1-7532

Date and time of death: 7/24/YR-1; 2123 **Place of death:** Nita Community Hospital

Date and time of exam: 7/25/YR-1; 1500

Identifying Characteristics: **Eyes:** Brown **Hair:** Brown **Height:** 72 in. **Weight:** 165 lbs.

The cause of death is found to be:

Immediate cause: EXSANGUINATING HEMORRHAGE

Due to: SEVERED INNOMINATE ARTERY

Due to: GUNSHOT TO CHEST

Circumstances of Death

This thirty-seven-year-old male was involved in an altercation in which he was allegedly shot with a large caliber weapon. Evidently there were attempted cardiopulmonary resuscitation efforts made at the scene. He was removed by ambulance to Nita Community Hospital where he was pronounced dead.

The autopsy was performed the next day after x-rays had been taken at Nita Community Hospital. The autopsy was performed at the Darrow County Coroner's Office.

Pathologist

Leslie LoMonico, MD

Others Present at Autopsy

From the Darrow County Sheriff's Office: Inspector Jamie Stanton

From the Coroner's Division: Sergeant Scott Hill

From the District Attorney's Office: Investigator T. J. Leach

Initial Examination

The body is examined on a gurney at the Darrow County morgue. The body is clothed, although the shirt has been partially removed, evidently during the cardiopulmonary resuscitative efforts. The shirt is a light-blue denim work shirt with snap buttons. It is blood soaked over the front, back, left side, right side, and sleeves. The sleeves are short. There is in the upper left-hand pocket a blue, felt-tip pen and a folded piece of paper with writing on it. The shirt is labeled "machine wash warm, tumble dry, permanent press." There is a small tear in the fabric at the left edge of the button placket. This is just above the top-most button by a distance of approximately one inch. This has an opening of approximately five millimeters. If the shirt had been buttoned, the defect would have been approximately aligned with the entrance wound as described below. No other defects are detected.

The lower portion of the body is covered by blue denim jeans, which are secured with a brown leather belt and a brass belt closure. The jeans show a right rear pocket label reading "Lee." The belt has bloodstains over the posterior portion of it on the right. There is also some staining on the pant legs both right and left, in an irregular distribution. No holes are detected on examination. The pockets are not examined. Under the jeans are jockey-type briefs, dark blue in color, and without evidence of injury or tear.

The feet are covered by gray-white cotton socks and by brown leather cowboy boots, which rise to above the ankles approximately to the level of the top of his socks. The boots are somewhat bloodstained over the toes. All clothing is submitted to Inspector Stanton. After the clothing is removed, the body is examined.

External Examination

The body is that of a well-developed, well-nourished male who appears the age of thirty-seven years or younger. The body has been refrigerated and is cold to the touch. Fully fixed rigor mortis is present in the jaw, torso, and extremities. A fixed posterior lividity pattern is present. The body is unembalmed.

Prior to washing, the face shows an irregular distribution of dried, caked blood mainly on the cheeks, nose, and area of the mouth. There are linear streaks that run in an anterior-posterior direction consistent with running from the mouth while lying on his back. There is also some fine, caked blood over the upper portion of the chest and the upper extremities. This is an irregular distribution. There is also some blood on the abdomen and chest. This is a fine, dried, caked material. No other bloodstain patterns are seen. The body is washed of obscuring blood prior to further examination.

The subject is normocephalic. The head is covered with long brown hair, which has a normal male pattern of distribution. There is gravel and other debris within the hair admixed with dried, caked blood. No external trauma of the face or scalp is seen. The eyes are brown, the pupils are equal and dilated. The conjunctivae and sclerae are clear. The ears, nose, and throat are unremarkable. There is no fracture identified.

The chest is symmetrically formed. A penetrating wound is present on the upper chest; the wound is described in detail below. No palpable crepitance or bony deformity is noted over the chest wall. The abdomen is flat and firm; no external trauma is seen. No abdominal masses are palpable. The external genitalia are normal circumcised adult male. The testes are palpably unremarkable. The anus is closed and atraumatic.

The upper extremities are symmetrically formed, without evidence of injury. There is dried blood over the forearms, hands, and dorsal surface of the right hand. The lower extremities are normally formed and atraumatic. The back is symmetrical and is without visible injury.

Evidence of Trauma

A penetrating gunshot wound of the upper chest is present.

Entrance Wound

There is a gunshot entrance wound centered fourteen inches below the top of the head; this is also noted to be half an inch above the sternal notch; the central portion of the defect is one inch to the left of the midline. This is immediately above the sternoclavicular junction. The defect is oblong with a horizontal orientation. It is one inch in length, including an abrasion collar at the margins of the wound. The width of the wound is half an inch. The wound orientation and the presence of an elongated abrasion collar at the left margin suggest a left-to-right direction of the entering projectile. The right edge of the wound shows undermining of the underlying subcutaneous tissue.

Surrounding the wound there is contusion with grayish-blue discoloration of the skin. This extends for a distance of approximately half an inch at maximum, predominately to the right of the wound defect with a minimal amount to the left. The wound edges show no searing. They are smooth, pink, and soft. There is no evidence of soot deposition or stippling about the wound edges.

Slightly superior and to the right of the entrance wound are three vertically oriented defects in the skin surface. These are superficial and extend only to the epidermis on gross examination. They average one-quarter to one-half inch in length. The lower two defects are about one inch from the central portion of the wound, and the upper one is approximately two inches from the center of the wound and on a line with the center of the wound from the tip of the chin.

After the wound edges are cleaned, there is no significant alteration to the description as given above. The only exception is that to the right of the entrance defect there is a superficial incised wound that extends only through the epithelium. This is consistent with a cut originating from the jewelry that was in place.

Visible within the defect is a white metallic fragment, which appears to be a portion of jewelry. The fragment is removed; it appears to be a piece of jewelry. It has two arms or wings with some scroll work carving along them. These join in a central piece that appears incomplete and apparently is fractured. The arms measure approximately one inch. The piece is approximately three-quarters of an inch in greatest width. This is passed to Inspector Stanton.

Exit Wound

No exit wound is present. Postmortem radiographs show a retained radiopaque projectile overlying the right scapular tip, apparently external to the right chest cavity. Dissection in the area reveals a deformed bullet described below. The bullet is lodged six inches to the right of the midline and about twelve inches below the top of the head.

Path of Projectile

A hemorrhagic wound track is traced from the entrance defect into the upper right chest cavity. The wound track perforates the innominate artery and extends into the upper lobe of the right lung. The right upper lobe is perforated. The wound path exits the right chest cavity through the posterolateral third rib and lodges in the external chest wall at the tip of the right scapula.

Recovery of Projectile

A deformed bullet is removed from the posterior chest wall as noted above. It measures eighteen millimeters in diameter by eighteen millimeters in length. The anterior portion is flattened. The base of the projectile also appears deformed. My initials, "LL," are inscribed on the base, and the bullet is passed off to Inspector Stanton.

Direction of Travel

The wound path through the body is directed front to back, slightly upward, and left to right. The wound path is at an angle of approximately 40 degrees from the coronal plane.

Blunt Trauma

Over the forehead, immediately above the angle of the left eyebrow is a small ovoid cutaneous abrasion, one-quarter inch in length and diagonally oriented. Posterior to this by approximately three inches and within the hairline there are three similar abrasions. Two of the abrasions are elongated and vertically oriented. The third is linear and horizontally oriented. These are consistent with a fall and striking the ground.

Internal Examination

The body is opened with a standard Y-shaped trunk incision. The subcutaneous fat thickness is about one inch at mid abdomen. Reflection of the chest plate reveals a right hemothorax consisting of approximately 900 milliliters of liquid and partially clotted blood. The right lung is collapsed. The left chest cavity is free of blood or excess fluid. No pleural adhesions are present. The pericardial sac is intact, thin, and smooth and contains about ten milliliters of clear straw-colored serous fluid. The peritoneal surfaces are smooth and glistening; no adhesion or fluid accumulation is noted in the abdominal cavity. The internal organs are normally arranged.

Heart

The heart is in normal position. It weighs 275 grams. Its surface is smooth. There is a small amount of epicardial fat. The coronary vessels are unremarkable. They are patent throughout their entire length. On cut surface the myocardium is red-brown and without evidence of fibrosis or acute infarction. The ventricular walls are normal in thickness. The cardiac chambers are not dilated. The endocardial surfaces are normal. The valves are normally formed with thin, smooth pliable leaflets.

The aortic outflow tract shows a laceration of the innominate artery one centimeter distal to its origin, secondary to the bullet wound. The laceration involves the anterior portion of the artery for a length of two-and-a-half to three centimeters. The posterior surface of the innominate is intact. The other major vessels are unremarkable.

Lungs

Right lung shows perforating trauma as described above. Left lung is unremarkable. The surface is tan-pink, smooth, and without nodularity. The bronchial and vascular trees are unremarkable.

Abdominal Organs

The abdominal organs are normal for the age of the patient. There is no significant change.

Adrenals

The adrenal glands are moderately small. Representative samples are taken.

Central Nervous System

The central nervous system is examined. There is no evidence of edema, or of tumor or infection.

Toxicology

Representative samples of blood from the right chest, urine, bile, and gastric contents are taken for toxicology.

Organ Samples Saved

Representative samples of all organs are saved, as well as the skin wound, the tract through the lung and the innominate artery.

Cause Of Death

Exsanguinating hemorrhage due to a severed innominate artery due to a gunshot wound to the chest.

Other Significant Condition

Gunshot penetration of the upper lobe of the right lung.

Three separate diagrams of the wound path are prepared and attached at the end of this report.

_____
Leslie LoMonico, MD, Pathologist

NAME: Abbott, Donald   DATE: 7/25/YR-1   CASE NUMBER: YR-1 - 134

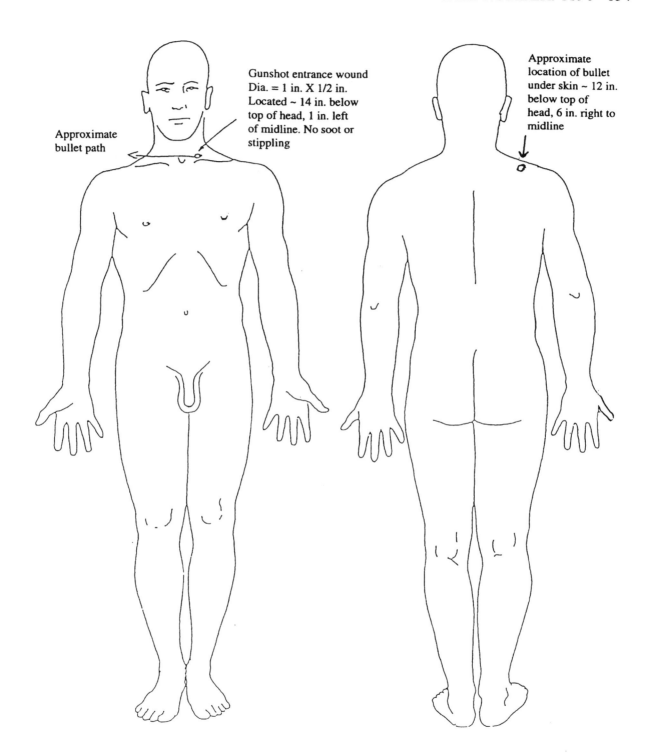

Gunshot entrance wound
Dia. = 1 in. X 1/2 in.
Located ~ 14 in. below
top of head, 1 in. left
of midline. No soot or
stippling

Approximate
bullet path

Approximate
location of bullet
under skin ~ 12 in.
below top of
head, 6 in. right to
midline

NAME: Abbott, Donald   DATE: 7/25/YR-1   CASE NUMBER: YR-1 - 134

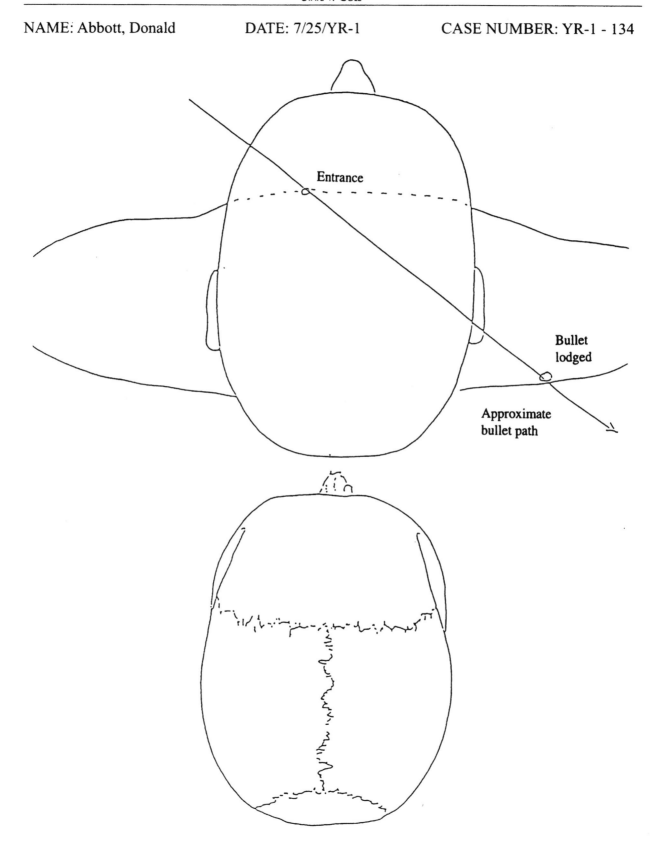

Entrance

Bullet
lodged

Approximate
bullet path

NAME: Abbott, Donald   DATE: 7/25/YR-1   CASE NUMBER: YR-1 - 134

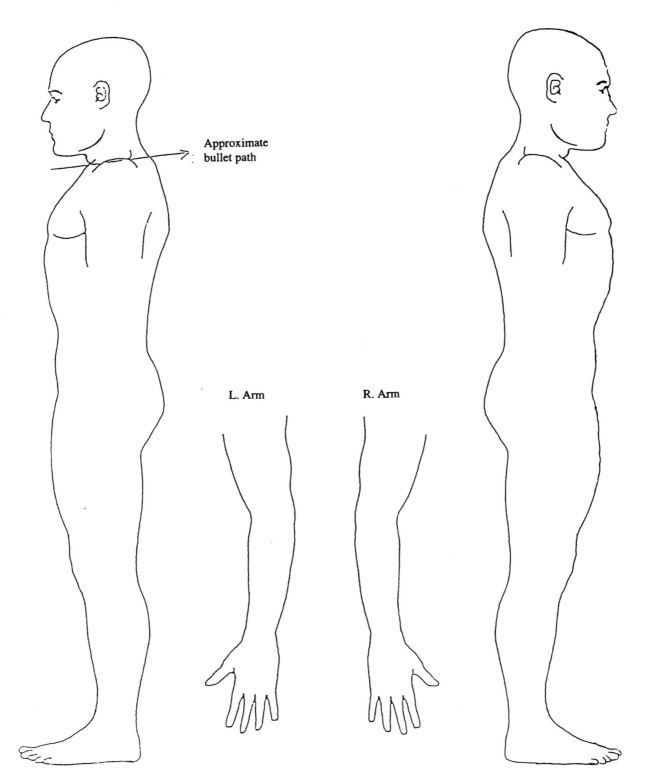

Approximate
bullet path

L. Arm   R. Arm

NITA DEPARTMENT OF JUSTICE
INVESTIGATIVE SERVICES BRANCH
PHYSICAL EVIDENCE EXAMINATION REPORT

TO: Darrow County Sheriff's Office,   **Attn:** Inspector Jamie Stanton

TYPE OF CASE: Homicide

SUBJECTS: Cole, Walter (Suspect); Abbott, Donald (Victim)

DATE OF REPORT: August 7, YR-1

A telephone request was received by the undersigned from the Darrow County Sheriff's Office on July 25, YR-1, at approximately 1000 hours regarding the examination of a vehicle and other evidence involved in a homicide. I arrived at the DCSO at 1115 hours and was informed of the details of the homicide and the nature of the examination requested. I was shown a Chevrolet Blazer, Nita license 2UDE900. I was informed that I would receive additional evidence from Inspector Stanton after the completion of the autopsy, which was scheduled later that afternoon.

The driver's door of the Blazer was examined for fingerprints. Two usable latent impressions were developed as follows:

> A usable latent impression was developed on the outside of the driver's door on the door handle.

> A usable latent impression was developed on the driver's sideview mirror.

The driver's door around the window frame was also examined for the presence of gunpowder residue. Examination of the vehicle was completed by 1145 hours.

Later that afternoon, at approximately 1700 hours, Inspector Stanton delivered the following items of evidence to me at my office in Nita City:

> Item 1: One .38 caliber Smith & Wesson revolver, serial number 5K85357.

> Item 2: A sealed bag containing five (5) .38 Special Remington-Peters cartridges.

> Item 3: A sealed plastic vial containing one lead bullet.

> Item 4: A sealed plastic bag containing a damaged piece of jewelry.

> Item 5: A small glass vial containing blood.

> Item 6: Clothing of the victim, including:

>> A. One heavily bloodstained blue shirt.

>> B. One pair of blue jeans.

>> C. One pair of blue undershorts.

>> D. One pair of boots

> Item 7: A card containing the known fingerprints of Donald Abbott.

> Item 8: A card containing the known fingerprints of Walter Cole.

Analysis

1. Neither of the latent fingerprints were made by Donald Abbott. The print found on the driver's door handle was made by the left middle finger of Walter Cole. The print from the sideview mirror was not made by either Donald Abbott or Walter Cole.

2. The weapon (Item 1) was examined, test fired, and found to be functioning properly. Trigger pull was four (4) pounds single-action and ten (10) pounds double-action, normal for both modes of firing on a Smith & Wesson revolver.

3. The bullet (Item 3) exhibits class characteristics similar to those of the submitted revolver (Item 1) and could have been fired from that revolver. There is insufficient individual detail present on the bullet to demonstrate positively that the submitted revolver did or did not fire the bullet.

4. Some gunpowder residue was detected on the shirt (Item 6A). However, no significant pattern of gunpowder residue was observed that would allow a muzzle-to-victim distance to be determined. The lack of pattern may be attributable to either heavy bloodstaining on the shirt or to a distance of approximately four (4) feet between victim and weapon muzzle.

5. Gunpowder residue was detected on the window frame of the driver's door of the Chevrolet Blazer, license number 2UDE900.

Disposition

Inspector Stanton was notified by telephone of the results of the analysis on August 5, YR-1, at 1430 hours. Inspector Stanton retrieved all items of evidence previously given to me on August 6, YR-1, at 1000 hours.

Jan Newman

Jan Newman
Criminalist
Nita DOJ

Arrest and Conviction Record of Donald Franklin Abbott

RE: STANTON, J., DCSO   **DATE:** 7/25/YR-1 **TIME:** 0935

CIR: A3639220

DOB: 03/20/YR-38 **SEX:**M

NAM: 01 ABBOTT, DONALD FRANKLIN

NDL: S2662492

SSN: 565238199

****

ARR/DET/CITE/CONV:

1

11/27/YR-11 ARREST LEWISTON (ID) PD, C.C. 1751, POSS. OF DRUGS W/ INTENT TO SELL

03/05/YR-10 PG NEZ PERCE DIST. CT, C.C. 1752, POSS. OF DRUGS (FELONY). SENTENCE: 3 YEARS PROBATION, 30 DAYS CO. JAIL (WEEKENDS)

****

2

01/03/YR-4 ARREST DCSO, V.C. 1530, RECKLESS DRIVING

01/15/YR-4 PG DARROW JUST. CT, V.C. 1530, RECKLESS DRIVING (MISD). SENTENCE: $250 FINE

****

NOT TO BE DUPLICATED

Arrest and Conviction Record of Walter Joseph Cole

RE: STANTON, J., DCSO   **DATE:** 7/25/YR-1 **TIME:** 0938

CIR: A2940894

DOB: 10/05/YR-41 **SEX:** M

NAM: 01 COLE, WALTER JOSEPH

        02 COLE, WALLY

NDL: R4449845

SSN: 562837947

****

ARR/DET/CITE/CONV:

#1

05/03/YR-7 APPLICATION TO NITA COMMUNITY HOSPITAL, FINGERPRINTS SUBMITTED, DCSO

****

NOT TO BE DUPLICATED

TESTIMONY OF PAT MILLER AT PRELIMINARY HEARING
October 16, YR-1

Direct Examination (by the prosecution)

I am a Darrow County deputy sheriff. I have been in the sheriff's department for eight years, all of them as a patrol officer. On July 24, YR-1, I was on patrol in Apple Valley and Highlands Vista. I was on Highlands Vista Road going towards Glenwood Canyon Road. At approximately 1955 hours (7:55 p.m.) I received a call from my dispatcher about a possible shooting on Glenwood Canyon Road at the Community Church. As I responded Code 3, I was informed by radio that the rescue squad from the fire department had also been dispatched. As I was proceeding down Glenwood Canyon I saw the rescue squad pull out of the fire department and disappear over the hill leading to the Community Church.

I arrived at the scene at approximately 8:02 p.m. Two EMTs appeared to be giving CPR to a man lying on the ground who was later identified as Donald Abbott. A third EMT was leading another man away from the man on the ground to a black and silver Blazer with a trailer. I was informed by Jason Svoboda, EMT, that Mr. Abbott did not appear to have any vital signs and that an ambulance would arrive momentarily. I told Svoboda to have Mr. Abbott taken to the nearest emergency room at Nita Community Hospital. I was also told that as the EMTs arrived they observed Mr. Cole performing CPR on Mr. Abbott.

Deputies Warren and Padilla arrived. I asked them to coordinate with the EMTs and preserve the crime scene. A few minutes later Sergeant Kapandritis arrived and took charge. At approximately 8:20 p.m. Inspector Stanton from our homicide unit arrived and took charge. Meanwhile, I had gone over to the man at the Blazer. I asked for identification, and he told me he was Wally Cole and that he lived right behind the church. I asked him if he had shot the other man, and he said yes. I asked him where the gun was, and he said, "In the Blazer." I looked in the Blazer through the open driver's door and saw what appeared to be a .38 police special sticking up between the driver's seat and the console. I closed the door and moved Mr. Cole over to my patrol car.

Standing at the rear of my car, I advised Mr. Cole of his *Miranda* rights. He said that he was aware of them and that he was willing to tell me what happened. He told me that he had had an affair with the wife of the man he had shot. The affair had ended in January, and shortly after that the victim, who he identified as Don Abbott, had learned of the affair. Abbott threatened to kill Cole on several occasions and apparently tried to accomplish it on several occasions. Once, according to Cole, Abbott had found Cole parked at the Standard Station in town and had threatened to kill him. On another time Abbott had chased Cole all through Apple Valley, and on still another occasion Abbott had gotten in front of Cole and had actually driven up Cole's driveway.

That night Cole and his wife had taken their ATV into Nita City to be repaired and were returning home towing their trailer. Abbott came speeding by him and then pulled in front and braked sharply, almost coming to a complete stop. Abbott signaled for Cole to pull over, but Cole refused. As they reached the fire station, Abbott sped up and disappeared over the hill. As Cole came down the hill and turned into his driveway, he found himself blocked by Abbott's Toyota pickup. He saw Abbott walking rapidly around the truck and coming towards the Blazer, waving his arms around. Abbott came up to the pickup and said, "Your time is now." Abbott reached through the window with both arms when Cole shot him. Cole said he then attempted to give CPR to Abbott. I saw blood on Cole's hands, arms, and sleeves consistent with CPR.

Cole also told me that he had talked with an attorney about Abbott's threats and the attorney had advised Cole to carry a loaded gun with him at all times.

I did not see any blood either in the Blazer or on the exterior.

I recognize Exhibit 1 as a diagram of the Apple Valley/Highlands Vista area that I drew about two weeks ago at the request of the district attorney's office. It is reasonably accurate. I have placed an "X" at the approximate location of the killing. Exhibit 2 is a diagram of the scene that I drew on the morning of July 25. I did not place the vehicles on the diagram because we have photos that accurately show the positions of the vehicles, and they had been removed when I drew the diagram.

Exhibits 3, 4, 5, and 6 are photographs that I took at the scene on July 24. Exhibit 3 shows the two vehicles and the trailer. Exhibit 4 was taken more closely to the vehicles and does not show the trailer. Exhibit 5 shows the gun where I first saw it, looking through the passenger's door, and Exhibit 6 is a close up of the gun from the driver's door. Exhibit 7 is also a photograph of the same gun, but this was taken back at the sheriff's office in Nita after we had taken the gun into evidence. Exhibit 8 is a photograph I took two weeks ago, when I drew Exhibit 1. It shows Glenwood Canyon Road looking north from the top of the hill just past the fire station. It shows that you cannot see the driveway into the church parking lot from that position. Exhibit 9 was taken at the same time as the last exhibit. It was taken from the west side of Glenwood Canyon Road about halfway down the hill. It shows the entrance to the driveway and the sign for the Community Church.

Cross-Examination (by the defense)

I took no notes at the scene, and I did not tape record the statement I took from Mr. Cole. I wrote the report from memory on the morning of July 25. I believe that the report is accurate, but I could be mistaken about the number of chases that Mr. Cole described. I thought he said that the incident at the service station and the chase through Apple Valley were two different times, but I could be wrong about that.

I am not wrong about his description of the killing. I remember very clearly asking how Abbott approached the Blazer, and I demonstrated what I thought was his response. Mr. Cole said "no" and then did his own demonstration, putting both hands straight forward from his shoulders. [The Court notes that the witness has demonstrated by putting both arms straight out from his shoulders while sitting in the witness chair.] Mr. Cole did say that Mr. Abbott's right hand was always behind him, so that he could not see if Abbott was holding anything in that hand, but at another time he said that Abbott was waving both hands around in the air.

Mr. Cole was always cooperative with me. He answered all my questions quickly and politely. I never felt that Mr. Cole presented any danger to me.

I am sure that Mr. Cole told me that his attorney had told him to carry a loaded gun with him at all times. I don't know why I did not include this in my report, but I remember it clearly because I thought it was strange advice to come from an attorney. He did not give me the name of the attorney, and I did not ask for it.

Diagram (Exhibit 1)

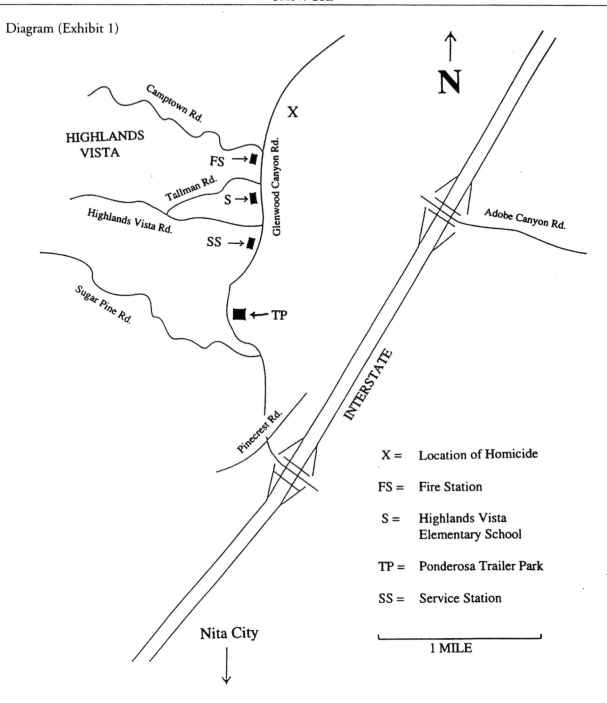

X = Location of Homicide

FS = Fire Station

S = Highlands Vista
Elementary School

TP = Ponderosa Trailer Park

SS = Service Station

1 MILE

Diagram of Highlands Vista and Apple Valley

PAT MILLER #170

Diagram (Exhibit 2)

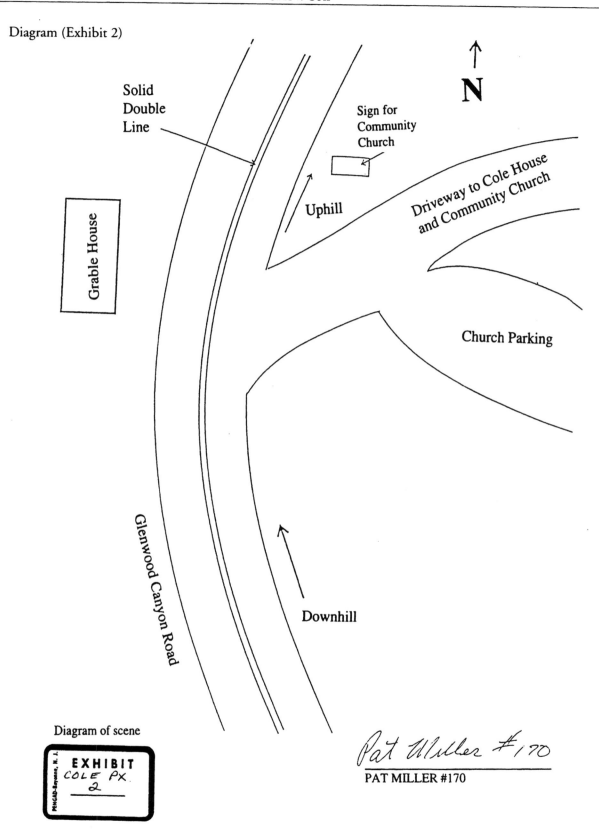

Solid Double Line

Sign for Community Church

N

Driveway to Cole House and Community Church

Uphill

Grable House

Church Parking

Glenwood Canyon Road

Downhill

Diagram of scene

EXHIBIT
COLE PX.
2
PRINGAD—Bayonne, N. J.

Pat Miller #170

PAT MILLER #170

Photo (Exhibit 3)

Photo (Exhibit 4)

Photo (Exhibit 5)

Photo (Exhibit 6)

Photo (Exhibit 7)

Photo (Exhibit 8)

Photo (Exhibit 9)

Testimony of Virginia Abbott at Preliminary Hearing
October 16, YR-1

Direct Examination (by the prosecution)

My correct name is Virginia Abbott, but everyone has called me Ginny since I was a small girl. I was married to Donald Abbott, and I have four minor children. I have now moved back near my parents in Medford, Oregon.

On July 24, YR-1, about 7:30 p.m. Don and I left our home in Don's Toyota pickup truck. Don was driving. We were going to the Nita Express yard in North Nita so that Don could pick up his truck. He was to pick up a load later that night and then deliver it up north. He was expecting to be on the road for at least three to four days.

As we were getting on the interstate at Glenwood Canyon Road, Don looked over to his left and saw Wally and Brenda in their Blazer. They were towing an empty trailer. Don slammed on the brakes and yelled, "I'm going to kill that son-of-a-bitch." I told Don to calm down, that he had to pick up a load that night so we had to be on our way. Don seemed to calm down and drove down the interstate for no more than a half mile when he again slammed on the brakes and pulled into the median strip. He again said that he would kill Wally, and he used a string of profanity that I don't like to hear. I kept saying, "Let's go on," but he wouldn't listen. He made a U-turn on the median strip and raced back north on the interstate, significantly exceeding the speed limit. I told him to let me out and I would wait at the Park-and-Ride when he was ready to return to the truck. He brought the pickup to a stop and yelled at me, "If you're going to get out, get out quickly." I did, and he drove off at a high rate of speed down Glenwood Canyon Road. I really didn't think he would catch Wally, so I expected him to come back and pick me up. Then I saw first a sheriff's car and then a highway patrol car get off the interstate and race up Glenwood Canyon with lights and sirens on. Shortly after that an ambulance followed with its lights and siren. By this time I thought there had been an accident, so I ran up the road to a friend's house and had her give me a ride.

I never found an accident, but when I got to the church driveway I saw Don's pickup and Wally's Blazer. Wally was standing by a sheriff's car, so I walked over to him. He told me, "It's all over, babe." Then a deputy asked me who I was, and Wally introduced me. The deputy told me that my husband had been taken to the hospital and that I should go there and wait to talk to a deputy sheriff.

Exhibits 3 and 4 are photographs of our Toyota pickup and Wally's Blazer.

Cross-Examination (by the defense)

Wally and I had an affair from YR-4 until January of this year. It was a mutual decision to break it off. After the affair ended, we continued to see each other two to three times a month, but just to talk; we have not had any sex since the affair ended. We talked about the threats my husband was making. I learned about the threats both from my husband and from Wally, and I told Wally about some of which he wasn't aware.

I learned of the first chase, through Apple Valley, when Don came home. He told me all about it and said he was real sorry that he hadn't caught Wally. He also told me about chasing Wally right up his driveway. He got a lot of pleasure telling me how he chased Wally right into his own house. I was afraid that Don would really hurt Wally, but Wally never said anything to me about being afraid of Don.

One time Don and I were driving in Nita City when we saw Wally and Brenda driving the other way. Don made a U-turn right in all that traffic, but by the time he could get turned around Wally had sped off. On another occasion, Don was driving in Nita City when he saw Wally's Blazer parked on Lincoln Way. He jumped out of the pickup and told me to get behind the wheel and park it. Then he waited for almost an hour, watching the Blazer. Finally, when Brenda got in and drove off he realized he had wasted our time, and he got back into the pickup and we went home.

Another time Don told me that he had gone to the hospital and waited outside for over an hour for Wally to come out, but Wally never did, and finally Don had to leave to pick up a load with his truck. I told Wally about both of these incidents before he shot Don.

I have a revolver that I keep in our bedroom. I used it for protection when Don was on the road. I don't think Don ever removed it from the house. He had his own revolver. He usually kept it in the truck for protection when he was driving, but sometimes he would bring it home with him between trips. I know that he did not have it with him on July 24, because I later found it locked in his truck at Nita Express.

Today I do not recall Don ever saying that he wanted to kill Wally, except on July 24, of course. Before that it seems to me that he said he wanted to get Wally, or to hurt or beat him. However, if on July 24 I told a sheriff's officer that Don said he wanted to kill Wally on earlier occasions, then that was my best recollection at the time, because I told Inspector Stanton the truth as best I knew it at the time.

Even before the affair ended I had told Wally that Don had beaten me in the past, but I had made it clear that this had occurred many years ago in Idaho and not since we have been in Nita.

Testimony of Leslie LoMonico, MD,
at Preliminary Hearing
October 17, YR-1

Direct Examination (by the prosecution)

I am presently a pathologist and director of the pathology laboratory of the Darrow County Coroner's Office in Nita City. I have been a pathologist with that office since YR-10 and have been director for the past four years.

I received my bachelor of science degree, with a major in biochemistry, from the University of Arizona in Tucson. I received my medical degree from Stanford Medical School in Palo Alto, California, and then completed a one-year internship at the University of California at Davis Medical Center. I then did a four-year residency in anatomical and clinical pathology at the University of Nita Hospital in Nita City. I joined the Darrow County Coroner's Office after completing my residency.

I am licensed to practice medicine in both Nita and California. I am certified by the American Board of Pathology in anatomical, clinical, and forensic pathology. I am also a Diplomate of the National Board of Medical Examiners. I have conducted well over 1,000 autopsies and have qualified as an expert witness on the cause of death and the circumstances surrounding death in over 100 cases.

I performed an autopsy on the body of Donald Abbott on July 25, YR-1.

[At this point the defense offered to stipulate that the court could consider Dr. LoMonico's report in evidence. The prosecutor agreed, and the stipulation was accepted by the court. The autopsy report was entered into evidence as Exhibit 10. The prosecution had no further questions on direct examination.]

Cross-Examination (by the defense)

I examined Mr. Abbott's clothes before removing them from his body. Visually, I could not detect any gunpowder on the shirt, nor did I see a lead wipe around what appeared to be the entrance wound. Based upon this, it is my opinion that the muzzle of the gun was between four to six feet from the body. On the other hand, if there was gunpowder on the shirt, the gun could have been as close as two feet. I am sure that the gun was not closer than two feet or I would have seen gunpowder on the shirt. In my opinion, it is unlikely that the bleeding on the shirt would mask the presence of any gunpowder that might be there.

I found and removed only one slug from the body. The mechanism of death was that Mr. Abbott bled to death. The bleeding was caused by the severed artery, caused by the bullet passing through the artery. The bullet might have been deflected slightly by hitting the jewelry Mr. Abbott was wearing, but the jewelry was very light so the deflection was slight, if at all. Had the bullet passed an inch to either side it would not have severed the artery, so it is possible that it would not have caused death.

The bullet path was front to back, and left to right at approximately a 45-degree angle. In my opinion, the left shoulder of the deceased was definitely closer to the gun muzzle than was the right shoulder. The bullet path was almost level, possibly very slightly down to up. This establishes the relative position of the gun to the body, but I cannot determine the actual angle of the gun unless I know the position of the body, which I don't know.

If the body was leaning forward at the time of the shooting, then the gun would have been pointing upward.

TESTIMONY OF JAN NEWMAN AT PRELIMINARY HEARING
October 17, YR-1

Direct Examination (by the prosecution)

I am a senior criminalist for the Nita Department of Justice. I joined the department in YR-15 as a criminalist and was promoted to senior criminalist in YR-10. I received my bachelor of science degree in chemistry from Carnegie Institute of Technology, and my master's from the University of Nita. My thesis concerned the application of scientific principles in criminal investigations of homicide cases.

Since joining the department I have received extensive additional training. When I first joined the department, I studied fingerprint investigation and comparison under Spiro Stathos, who was then considered the best fingerprint expert in the state. I received other on-the-job training in all aspects of criminalistics, including the examination and analysis of foreign substances such as blood and gunpowder as well as the examination and comparison of bullets and firearms. I have also taken courses in these subjects at the FBI Academy at Quantico, Virginia.

During the past eight years I have taught in all of these fields at the Nita State Police Academy, and I have also lectured at various professional conferences. I have authored over a dozen articles, which have appeared in professional journals in my field, and I authored a chapter on fingerprint investigation and comparison in one of the leading textbooks on criminalistics.

I have testified as an expert witness in over one hundred cases in all areas of criminalistics in courts throughout Nita.

On July 25, YR-1, pursuant to a telephone call from the Darrow County Sheriff's Office, I examined a YR-5 Blazer, license plate 2UDE900, at the Sheriff's office in Nita City. My examination was conducted in three parts. First, I conducted a visual inspection of both the interior and exterior of the vehicle, looking for blood, gunpowder, and any visible fingerprints as well as anything else of possible evidentiary value. The results of the visual inspection were negative for all evidence.

Next, I conducted an examination for foreign substances not visible to the naked eye. I did this by taking seven swabs from around the window frame of the driver's door. Analysis of the swabs revealed that two samples contained small amounts of gunpowder. No blood was found in any of the samples.

Finally, I examined the exterior of the driver's side for fingerprints. Latent #1 was found on the driver's door handle. Latent #2 was found on the driver's outside rearview mirror.

Later, on July 25, I received a number of items of evidence at my office from DCSO Inspector Stanton. I conducted a number of examinations on these items of evidence. The Smith & Wesson .38 caliber revolver, serial number 5K85357, was test fired in the DOJ firing range. It was in operating condition, with a four-pound trigger pull in the single-action mode and a ten-pound pull for double action. Single action means the hammer has been cocked manually before the trigger is pulled; double action means that the trigger pull both cocks the hammer and fires the gun.

I then compared the damaged bullet slug I received from Inspector Stanton with the known slug I obtained by test firing the weapon. The damaged slug was consistent in caliber with having been fired from the weapon. However, due to the damage to the slug I was unable to make a definite comparison. Therefore, all I can say is that the bullet might have been fired from this weapon, but I cannot say that it either was or wasn't fired from this gun.

I compared the latent fingerprints with known prints of Walter Cole and Donald Abbott, which I received from Inspector Stanton. Latent #1, taken from the door handle, was from the left middle finger of Walter Cole. Latent #2, from the side view mirror, was not made by either Mr. Cole or Mr. Abbott.

Some gunpowder residue was detected on the shirt. No significant pattern of gunpowder residue was observed that would allow a muzzle-to-victim distance to be determined. The lack of pattern may be attributable to either heavy bloodstaining on the shirt or to a distance of approximately four feet between the victim and the weapon muzzle.

Cross-Examination (by the defense)

In no case in which I testified did the court ever determine that I was not qualified as an expert witness. It is true, however, that in one case in Jefferson County in YR-11 the judge found that my methodology did not meet scientific standards and he excluded my testimony on that basis. I, of course, totally disagree with that finding. However, the case did not go up on appeal, so we were not able to challenge that finding.

The trigger pulls on the gun are within normal limits for a weapon of this type. I found no evidence that the mechanism had been tampered with in any way to lessen the trigger pull. It certainly was not what we would call a "hair trigger." In my opinion, an adult male of average strength would be able to pull the trigger rather easily, even in the double action mode. I can't say whether the fear or excitement of being under attack would allow the shooter to pull the trigger without being conscious of doing so.

It is possible that I detected all the gunpowder that was on the front of the shirt. In that case, the gun muzzle would have been at least four feet from the deceased. On the other hand, it is possible that the large amount of blood on the shirt masked some of the gunpowder. In that case, the gun muzzle could have been as close as two feet. From a scientific viewpoint, either possibility is as reasonable as the other. The gunpowder was found on the left shoulder near the collar and also on the right shoulder.

I also conducted an analysis of a sample of blood, which I understand was drawn from Mr. Cole on the night of the shooting. The results of my analysis were negative for the presence of either alcohol or drugs.

The blood on the shirt was O positive. I did not do any further testing on this blood. Both Mr. Cole and Mr. Abbott had O positive blood, which is the most common type. Since I was not aware of any allegation that Mr. Cole was bleeding, I simply assumed that the blood on the shirt came from Mr. Abbott, but from a scientific position I cannot prove that.

As far as the gunpowder found on the Blazer, I found the traces in two of the seven samples I took. I did not mark each of the samples from the exact location on the window frame, so I am unable to say exactly where on the frame I found the gunpowder.

Testimony of Brenda Cole at Preliminary Hearing
October 18, YR-1

Direct Examination (by the defense)

I married Walter Cole in YR-17. We have three children—aged fifteen, thirteen, and eleven—who live with us. On July 24 we lived on Glenwood Canyon Road behind the Community Church.

In January of this year I learned from an anonymous telephone call that Wally had been having an affair with Ginny Abbott. When I confronted him, he admitted it but said that it had already ended and that he hoped I would forgive him and remain married to him. I wasn't so sure and suggested that we separate for a while until I could collect my thoughts. However, he never did move out.

A short time later, perhaps a week or so, he came home late one night upset and scared. He told me that Don Abbott had threatened to kill him and had chased him all over Apple Valley. Wally said that he was concerned that Abbott would try to kill him again. We agreed that it would not be a good idea for Wally to move out at that time.

A couple of weeks later, I was in the kitchen when I heard Wally driving very fast up the driveway. I looked out the window as Wally pulled up to the front door. I saw a black pickup truck that I did not recognize about halfway up the driveway. It looked just like the truck that Mr. Abbott was driving on July 24. Wally said that Abbott had again chased him down Glenwood Canyon Road, and he again said that he was afraid that Abbott would try to kill him.

One day in May or June Wally was driving the Blazer in Nita City, and I was in the front passenger seat. Suddenly Wally sped up and made a couple of sharp turns. I asked him what he was doing, and he said that Abbott had seen us and was trying to make a U-turn. I looked around, but I never saw Abbott on that occasion.

On July 24 we had taken the ATV into Nita City to have it repaired. We stopped for a bite to eat and then went to an ice cream store and got a quart of ice cream for the kids. We drove up the interstate and got off at Glenwood Canyon Road. As we were going down the road, I heard a sudden noise and a pickup truck sped past us and then cut right in front of us. The man in the driver's seat was motioning for us to pull over, but Wally wouldn't do it. Wally said it was Abbott, and he was afraid to stop. Abbott slowed his truck to about five miles per hour, but with the trailer we couldn't get around him. Finally, when we got to the fire station Abbott suddenly sped up and disappeared over the hill. I thought it had ended.

When we got to our driveway Wally pulled in, but there was the pickup blocking our way. Wally slammed on the brakes, and we stopped about ten feet from the truck. This man was coming around the rear of the truck very fast. He looked very angry. He came right up to the driver's window and said, "You son-of-a-bitch, your time is up." I was screaming. Wally leaned right up against me. Suddenly, I heard a shot, and the man fell back. Wally told me to go to Fern's and call for help, so I did. From the time Wally began braking in the driveway to the time of the shot could not have been more than five to ten seconds.

After I called for help I stayed at Fern's house until the officer came and talked to me. After the shooting I did not talk to Wally until after I spoke with the officer. At the time I did not know that Ginny Abbott had come to the scene and spoken to my husband.

Cross-Examination (by the prosecution)

Wally and I are still living together, and I think we will continue to do so while this case is pending, but after that I just don't know. I'll deal with it when the time comes. I know the affair was mutual, but I still blame that woman for it; she knew there were children involved who would be hurt.

When Wally came home after the Apple Valley chase he said that Abbott had threatened to kill him, not just hurt him. I could tell that Wally was very frightened.

On July 24, when Abbott was driving about five miles per hour in front of us, Wally said, "This jerk is really asking for trouble." I did not ask him what he meant by that.

At no time did I ever see Donald Abbott with a weapon of any kind, either before July 24 or on that day. Nor did Wally ever tell me that he had seen Abbott with a gun.

I knew that Wally had a gun. We had used it when we went off-road. One time I remember Wally killing a rattlesnake with it. On July 24 I did not know that it was in the car. I never saw where Wally got the gun. The first time I saw it was when Wally fired it once. It scared me so much I almost jumped out of my skin.

I know that Abbott was right up against the car when the shot went off, but I don't remember where his hands were. I'm sorry, but I was so scared that my memory just isn't clear. My best guess is that the gun was one or two feet from Abbott when the shot was fired.

Before the shooting Wally never told me that Abbott had gone looking for him at the hospital.

Redirect Examination

On July 24 while we were driving down Glenwood Canyon Road, even while Abbott forced us to drive at five miles per hour, I did not see Wally take out the gun. Even though I did not see where or when he got it, I am sure that he did not have it in his hand when we first pulled into the driveway.

Testimony of Jamie Stanton at Preliminary Hearing
October 18, YR-1

Direct Examination (by the defense)

I am presently an Inspector in the Darrow County Sheriff's Office in charge of the Homicide/Assault Unit. I have been a law enforcement officer for over twenty years and have headed the Homicide Unit for approximately five years.

On July 24, YR-1, I was paged by DCSO dispatch and informed that a shooting had occurred in Highlands Vista at the Community Church. I responded immediately and was briefed by Sergeant Kapandritis and Deputy Miller.

Ultimately, I left the scene and went to Nita Community Hospital. I was informed that Donald Abbott had been pronounced dead. I was introduced to his widow, Virginia Abbott, who had been talking with a friend and a couple of nurses. Mrs. Abbott appeared to have been crying, but she was relatively calm and composed when I met her. I expressed sympathy on the death of her husband and informed her that it would help us understand what had happened if she could talk to me. She agreed to do so. A nurse said we could use one of the doctor's offices, so I took her into a small private office. I took extensive notes during the interview and reviewed them carefully when preparing my report.

Mrs. Abbott told me about her marriage to Donald Abbott and difficulties they had, particularly when they were living in Idaho. She told me that after moving to Nita she went to work in the admissions office of the hospital. It was here that she met Wally Cole. They had an affair from YR-4 until January of this year. Just after they had mutually ended the affair, Mrs. Cole had learned of it and called her one morning while Don was still at the house, so he learned of it as well. Within a week of the phone call Mr. Abbott came home one night and told her that he had found Wally parked by the school on Glenwood Canyon Road and had chased him all through Apple Valley. She asked her husband why he had done that, and he replied that he wanted to kill him.

A short time later, maybe a week or two, her husband came home and said that he had again chased Wally, this time right up the Cole driveway. He again said that he wanted to kill Cole, but he didn't want to do it where the children might see the killing. Mrs. Abbott didn't see either of these incidents and only knew what her husband and Wally had told her. She did have personal knowledge of two other incidents where Mr. Abbott tried, but failed, to catch Mr. Cole.

Mrs. Abbott said that she was concerned for Mr. Cole's safety. Even though the affair was over, they continued to see each other once or twice a month; they would simply talk. She told Mr. Cole about her husband's threats to kill him.

Cross-Examination (by the prosecution)

Mr. Abbott had not used or threatened any violence against her since they had moved to Nita. She told me that she knew her husband owned a handgun, but she never saw it that night. As far as she knew, it was still in the truck. Later that night we recovered Mr. Abbott's gun from the cab of his truck parked in the Nita Express yard in North Nita.

TESTIMONY OF WALTER COLE AT PRELIMINARY HEARING
October 18, YR-1

Direct Examination (by the defense)

[Defendant was informed by the court that he had a constitutional right to remain silent and not to take the witness stand at this hearing or the trial. Mr. Cole said that he understood this right and gave it up in order to testify. His counsel agreed with the waiver.]

I have been married to Brenda Cole for sixteen years; we have three minor children, all of whom live at home with us. On July 24, YR-1, I was, and still am, the supervising radiology technician at Nita Community Hospital. I have worked there for over six years.

In YR-4, Ginny Abbott came to work at the hospital, and later that year we began our affair. Many times we talked about getting divorces and marrying each other, but finally during the past holiday season we each decided that we didn't want to divorce our respective spouses, so in January we mutually agreed to end the affair. At least until July 24 we still liked each other and continued to see each other and talk to each other, but there was no sex.

It was really ironic that I was able to keep the affair from Brenda while it was going on, but right after it ended she learned about it. I had worked late the night before and slept in that morning. Fortunately, the kids were at school. When I awoke, Brenda was furious. I admitted it and told her it was all over. She wasn't sure if she wanted a divorce or a separation, or if we should stay together for the kids, but she remained angry, and finally she said she was going to call Ginny and tell her off. I asked her not to, but I couldn't control her. She called Ginny and was screaming into the phone, and by the time she finished she had calmed down.

I began looking for another place to stay, but we didn't want to tell the kids until we had to. If the kids were at home, I went by the school and used my cell phone. That's where I was about a week later, sitting in my Blazer checking some phone numbers, when suddenly Don Abbott appeared banging on my window. I was very glad that the window was up and the door was locked. I drove off as fast as I could, but he jumped into his pickup and followed me. He had yelled at me, "I'm going to kill you, you son-of-a-bitch," so I was frightened. I drove all over Apple Valley before I finally lost him. I wasn't sure if he knew where I lived, so I drove to the hospital. I asked Dr. Baxter to check the parking lot to see if the pickup was out there, and when it wasn't I went home. I told Brenda what had happened, and the next day I loaded my .38 and put it under the driver's seat.

About a week later I was driving home down Glenwood Canyon Road when suddenly Don Abbott appeared right behind me. He was right on my tail, blowing his horn and motioning for me to pull over. I sped up and stayed in the middle of the road so that he couldn't pass me. I pulled up to my front door and looked around and couldn't believe that he had pulled in over halfway up the driveway. Brenda was looking out the kitchen window and saw him backing down the driveway. I never took the gun out from under the seat.

During the next several months there were other incidents. Once when Brenda and I were driving in Nita City he passed us going the other way. I saw that he was trying to make a U-turn, so I took off real fast. Later Ginny told me that the traffic had been so heavy that it took him a while to turn around, and by the time he had, I had gotten away. Ginny also told me about another time in Nita City when they saw my Blazer. Don jumped out of his pickup and ordered Ginny to park it. He then waited where he could watch my car. That time, however, Brenda was using my car, and when she got in and drove away Don must have realized that he had wasted his time, and he got back into his pickup and left. Ginny told me that on each of these occasions Don had told her that he intended to kill me, which is why I put my gun in the car after the first time.

On July 24 I got off work a little early, so Brenda and I decided it would be a good time to take our ATV into the shop for repairs. I loaded it on our flatbed trailer and towed it into Nita City. After we left it off we stopped for dinner. Then we went next door and got some ice cream to take home. We then drove up the interstate and got off at Glenwood Canyon to go home.

As we were passing the trailer park I suddenly heard a loud noise and saw Abbott passing us at a very high rate of speed. I don't know where he came from because I had looked out the rearview mirror and had seen two other cars that I didn't recognize. Anyway, Abbott cut right in front of us and then slammed on his brakes. He slowed to something like two to five miles per hour and kept motioning with his hand for me to pull over. I had slowed so that I wouldn't hit him, but I wouldn't pull over. Brenda kept screaming, "Do something," so I said as calmly as I could, "What do you want me to do?" This went on for some time as we went down the road, and then as we got to the fire station Abbott suddenly pulled off at a high rate of speed and disappeared over the hill. I assumed he had gotten tired of it and had left. I don't remember telling Brenda that Abbott was asking for trouble. We came over the hill, and I pulled into the driveway we share with the church. Suddenly I saw him parked across the driveway so that I couldn't get to the house. I slammed on my brakes and brought the Blazer to a stop about ten feet from the pickup.

Brenda was screaming at the top of her voice, but I don't remember what, if anything, she was saying. I saw Abbott coming around the left rear side of the pickup. He was moving very fast and looked like he was mumbling something that I couldn't hear. His left hand was down by his side, and his right hand was out of sight behind his back. He ran right up to the driver's window and said, "You son-of-a-bitch, your time is now." He put his left arm through the window towards me. I leaned away towards Brenda and the passenger door. Suddenly I heard a shot, and he staggered back. My gun was in my hand, but I have no recollection of either getting it from under the seat or pulling the trigger.

I immediately put the gun down and got out. I told Brenda to go across the street and call for help. I went to Abbott where he was lying off the driveway in the gravel and dirt. He did not appear to be breathing, but I could feel a very weak carotid pulse. Using my shirt, I pressed down over the apparent wound to try to stop the bleeding. When I next checked I could not detect any pulse, so I began CPR chest compressions. It was probably not more than a minute or two but it seemed like forever before the rescue squad arrived.

When Abbott was running toward my car I didn't know what, if anything, he had in his right hand. I knew that he owned a gun and that he had threatened to kill me. I was scared to death that he would kill me and perhaps even Brenda. I did not want to kill him, and I feel terrible about Ginny and her kids. I hope that someday they will be able to forgive me.

I heard Officer Miller's testimony about my statement, and it is wrong. I never told the officer that Abbott put both arms in the window. I only saw the left arm come through the window. The right hand was always behind Abbott's back. I also told the officer that I was at the school, not the service station, when Abbott confronted me, and that this was the same time that he chased me through Apple Valley. I don't know why the officer thought it was two separate occasions.

The only time that Abbott was in front of me was on July 24. I never told the officer that Abbott was in front of me on any other day. Finally, I told the officer that I had consulted with an attorney, but I never said anything about the attorney advising me to carry a gun. That never came up between me and the attorney, so I would have had no reason to say it to Officer Miller.

Cross-Examination (by the prosecution)

Before January of this year I kept my gun unloaded and locked up at home. In January when I put the loaded gun in my Blazer, I did not know that it is illegal to carry a loaded gun inside a car. Even if I had known it I probably would have kept the gun there anyway. It was for my protection and that of my family. I have never had written permission from the Sheriff to carry a loaded gun in my car.

On July 24 I did not know for a fact whether or not Abbott had a gun with him, but I assumed that he did because of the threats he had made against me. I did not see Abbott get out of the pickup. When I first saw him he was coming around the left rear end of the truck. I could not see his right hand. He was moving very rapidly toward me—I can't say that it was a run, but it definitely was a fast walk.

I know that I must have reached under the seat to get the gun, because there is no other reasonable explanation how it got into my hand, but I just don't have any recollection of doing so. When I put the gun under the seat it was not cocked, so I assume that it was in the double action mode that was previously described by that criminalist that you called here the other day. I don't remember pulling the trigger, but I assume that I probably did so; another possibility is that I bumped my arm as I was leaning back and that set off the gun, but I don't remember that happening either. I have no reason to disagree with the expert that the trigger pull in the double action mode is ten pounds. I never did anything to the gun to change the trigger pull.

If I could have backed out of the driveway I probably could have gotten away from Abbott, at least that day. However, I couldn't back out fast enough. As soon as I brought the car to a halt I thought about backing out, but with the trailer attached it would have taken too much time. From the time I first saw the pickup parked in the driveway until the time the shot went off was probably no more than five to ten seconds; there simply wasn't enough time to get away.

No, I didn't continue to see Ginny just to rub it in to Brenda and Mr. Abbott. At first we met just to give each other moral support, but then later I wanted to obtain as much information about Mr. Abbott's intentions as I could. Once he threatened to kill me I thought I needed as much protection as I could get.

I'm not accusing Officer Miller of lying, and I know of no reason why the officer would have any animosity towards me. I'm simply saying that the officer was not accurate in reporting my statement.

I don't recall telling Dr. Baxter that if Abbott wanted trouble he would get it.

Redirect Examination

In the past when I had taken the gun along in the car it was never loaded until we got to our destination. I would often have the kids with us, and I didn't want an accident in the car. I never really gave any thought about it being illegal to carry a loaded gun in the car. The only reason I kept a loaded gun in the car after January was for my protection.

Applicable Nita Criminal Code Sections

Section 100. Homicide, Definition of terms

1. Homicide means the killing of a person by another.

2. Person, when referring to the victim of a homicide, means a human being who had been born and was alive at the time of the homicidal act.

3. The term "after deliberation" means not only intentionally, but also that the decision to commit the act has been made after the exercise of reflection and judgment concerning the act. An act committed after deliberation is never one that has been committed in a hastily or impulsively.

Section 101. First-degree murder

1. A person commits the crime of first-degree murder if, after deliberation and with the intent to cause the death of a person other than himself or herself, he or she causes the death of that person or of another person.

2. First-degree murder is a felony punishable by confinement in prison for twenty-five years to life.

Section 102. Second-degree murder

1. A person commits the crime of second-degree murder if:

    a. He or she intentionally, but not after deliberation, causes the death of a person; or
    b. With intent to cause serious bodily injury to a person other than himself or herself, he or she causes the death of that person or of another person.

2. Second degree murder is a felony punishable by confinement in prison for 15 to 50 years.

Section 103. Manslaughter

1. A person commits the crime of manslaughter if:

    a. He or she recklessly causes the death of a person; or
    b. He or she kills another person while committing a misdemeanor inherently dangerous to other people; or
    c. He or she intentionally, but not after deliberation, causes the death of a person, under circumstances where the act causing the death was performed upon a sudden heat of passion caused by a serious and highly provoking act of the intended victim, affecting the person killing sufficiently to excite an irresistible passion in a reasonable person. However, if between the provocation and the killing there is an interval sufficient for the voice of reason and humanity to be heard, the killing is murder.

2. Manslaughter is a felony punishable by confinement in prison for 5 to 15 years.

Section 104. Criminally negligent homicide

1. A person commits the crime of criminally negligent homicide, if:

    a. By conduct amounting to criminal negligence, he or she causes the death of a person; or
    b. He or she intentionally causes the death of a person, but believes in good faith that circumstances exist that would justify the killing, but the belief that such circumstances exist is unreasonable.

2. A person acts with criminal negligence when, through a gross deviation from the standard of care that a reasonable person would exercise, he or she fails to perceive a substantial and unjustifiable risk that a result will occur, or that a circumstance exists.

3. Criminally negligent homicide is a misdemeanor punishable by confinement in the county jail for up to one year, or by a fine up to $10,000, or both.

Section 512.   Self-defense

Homicide is justifiable and not unlawful when committed by a person when resisting any attempt to murder any person, or to commit a felony, or to do some great bodily injury upon any person. The circumstances must be sufficient to excite the fears of a reasonable person, and the person committing the killing must act under the influence of such fears alone.

Section 12031.   Carrying a loaded firearm in a public place

1. It is unlawful for any person to carry a loaded firearm on his or her person or in a vehicle while in any public place or any public street.

2. This section shall not apply to any law enforcement officer or anyone else who has written permission from the Sheriff of the county of residence to carry such a loaded firearm.

3. Violation of this section is a misdemeanor punishable by incarceration in the county jail not to exceed six months, or by a fine of $10,000, or both.

JURY INSTRUCTIONS
STATE OF NITA V. WALTER COLE

PART I. PRELIMINARY INSTRUCTIONS GIVEN PRIOR TO EVIDENCE

01.01 Introduction

You have been selected as jurors and have taken an oath to well and truly try this case.

During the progress of the trial there will be periods of time when the court recesses. During those periods of time, you must not talk to any of the parties, their lawyers, or any of the witnesses.

If any attempt is made by anyone to talk to you concerning the matters here under consideration, you should immediately report that fact to the court.

You should keep an open mind. You should not form or express an opinion during the trial and should reach no conclusion in this case until you have heard all of the evidence, the arguments of counsel, and the final instructions as to the law that will be given to you by the court.

01.02 Conduct of the Trial

First, the attorneys will have an opportunity to make opening statements. These statements are not evidence and should be considered only as a preview of what the attorneys expect the evidence will be.

Following opening statements, witnesses will be called to testify. They will be placed under oath and questioned by the attorneys. Documents and other tangible exhibits may also be received as evidence. If an exhibit is given to you to examine, you should examine it carefully, individually, and without any comment.

It is counsel's right and duty to object when testimony or other evidence is being offered that he or she believes is not admissible.

When the court sustains an objection to a question, the jurors must disregard the question and the answer if one has been given and draw no inference from the question or answer or speculate as to what the witness would have said if permitted to answer. Jurors must also disregard evidence stricken from the record.

When the court sustains an objection to any evidence, the jurors must disregard that evidence. When the court overrules an objection to any evidence, the jurors must not give that evidence any more weight than if the objection had not been made.

When the evidence is completed, the attorneys will make final statements. These final statements are not evidence but are given to assist you in evaluating the evidence. The attorneys are also permitted to argue in an attempt to persuade you to a particular verdict. You may accept or reject those arguments as you see fit.

Finally, just before you retire to consider your verdict, I will give you further instructions on the law that applies to this case.

Part II. Final Instructions

1.00   Respective Duties of Judge and Jury

Ladies and Gentlemen of the Jury:

You have heard all the evidence and the arguments of the attorneys, and now it is my duty to instruct you on the law. You must arrive at your verdict by unanimous vote applying the law, as you are now instructed, to the facts as you find them to be.

The law applicable to this case is stated in these instructions, and it is your duty to follow all of them. You must not single out certain instructions and disregard others.

It is your duty to determine the facts and to determine them only from the evidence in this case. You are to apply the law to the facts and in this way decide the case. You must not be governed or influenced by sympathy or prejudice for or against any party in this case. Your verdict must be based on evidence and not upon speculation, guess, or conjecture.

From time to time the court has ruled on the admissibility of evidence. You must not concern yourselves with the reasons for these rulings. You should disregard questions and exhibits that were withdrawn or to which objections were sustained.

You should also disregard testimony and exhibits that the court has refused or stricken.

The evidence that you should consider consists only of the witnesses' testimony and the exhibits the court has received.

Any evidence that was received for a limited purpose should not be considered by you for any other purpose.

You should consider all the evidence in the light of your own observations and experiences in life.

Neither by these instructions nor by any ruling or remark that I have made do I mean to indicate any opinion as to the facts or as to what your verdict should be.

1.01   Credibility of Witnesses

You are the sole judges of the credibility of the witnesses and of the weight to be given to the testimony of each witness. In determining what credit is to be given any witness, you may take into account the witness's ability and opportunity to observe; his or her manner and appearance while testifying; any interest, bias, or prejudice the witness may have; the reasonableness of the testimony considered in the light of all the evidence; and any other factors that bear on the believability and weight of the witness's testimony.

1.02   Direct and Circumstantial Evidence

The law recognizes two kinds of evidence: direct and circumstantial. Direct evidence proves a fact directly; that is, the evidence by itself, if true, established the fact. Circumstantial evidence is the proof of facts or circumstances that give rise to a reasonable inference of other facts; that is, circumstantial evidence proves a fact indirectly in that it follows from other facts or circumstances according to common experience and observations in life. An eyewitness is a common example of direct evidence, whereas human footprints are circumstantial evidence that a person was present.

The law makes no distinction between direct and circumstantial evidence as to the degree or amount of proof required, and each should be considered according to whatever weight or value it may have. All of the evidence should be considered and evaluated by you in arriving at your verdict.

1.03 "Willfully" Defined

The word "willfully" when applied to the intent with which an act is done or omitted means with a purpose or willingness to commit the act or to make the omission in question. The word "willfully" does not require any intent to violate the law, or to injure another, or to acquire any advantage.

2.01 Information

The information in this case is the formal method of accusing the defendant of a crime and placing him on trial. It is not any evidence against the defendant and does not create any inference of guilt. The State has the burden of proving beyond a reasonable doubt every essential element of the crime charged in the information or any of the crimes included therein.

2.02 Presumption of Innocence

The defendant is presumed to be innocent of the charges against him. This presumption remains with him throughout every stage of the trial and during your deliberations on the verdict. The presumption is not overcome until, from all the evidence in the case, you are convinced beyond a reasonable doubt that the defendant is guilty.

2.03 Burden of Proof

The State has the burden of proving the guilt of the defendant beyond a reasonable doubt, and this burden remains on the State throughout the case. The defendant is not required to prove his innocence.

2.04 Reasonable Doubt

Reasonable doubt means a doubt based upon reason and common sense that arises from a fair and rational consideration of all the evidence or lack of evidence in this case. It is a doubt that is not a vague, speculative, or imaginary doubt, but such a doubt as would cause reasonable persons to hesitate to act in matters of importance to themselves.

2.05 Weighing Conflicting Testimony

You are not bound to decide an issue of fact in accordance with the testimony of a number of witnesses, which does not convince you, as against the testimony of a lesser number or other evidence, which appeals to your mind with more convincing force. You may not disregard the testimony of the greater number of witnesses merely from caprice, whim, or prejudice, or from a desire to favor one side against the other. You must not decide an issue by the simple process of counting the number of witnesses who have testified on the opposing sides. The final test is not in the relative number of witnesses, but in the convincing force of the evidence.

2.06 Motive

Motive is not an element of the crime charged and need not be shown. However, you may consider motive or lack of motive as a circumstance in this case. Presence of motive may tend to establish guilt. Absence of motive may tend to establish innocence. You will therefore give its presence or absence, as the case may be, the weight to which you find it to be entitled.

2.07 Defendant Not Testifying—No Inference of Guilt May Be Drawn

A defendant in a criminal trial·has a constitutional right not to be compelled to testify. You must not draw any inference from the fact that a defendant does not testify. Further, you must neither discuss this matter nor permit it to enter into your deliberations in any way.

2.08 Admission Defined

An admission is a statement made by the defendant other than at his trial that does not by itself acknowledge his guilt of the crime for which he is on trial, but which statement tends to prove his guilt when considered with the rest of the evidence.

You are the exclusive judges as to whether the defendant made an admission, and if so, whether such statement is true in whole or in part. If you should find that the defendant did not make the statement, you must reject it. If you find that it is true in whole or in part, you may consider that part which you find to be true.

2.09 Expert testimony

A person is qualified to testify as an expert if he or she has special knowledge, skill, experience, training, or education sufficient to qualify him or her as an expert on the subject to which his or her testimony relates.

You are not bound to accept an expert opinion as conclusive, but you should give to it the weight to which you find it to be entitled. You may disregard any such opinion if you find it to be unreasonable.

3.00 Charges

The State of Nita has charged the defendant, Walter Cole, with the crime of first degree murder, which includes the crimes of second-degree murder, manslaughter, and criminally negligent homicide. If you are not satisfied beyond a reasonable doubt that the defendant is guilty of the crime charged, you may nevertheless convict the defendant of any lesser crime, if you are convinced beyond a reasonable doubt that the defendant is guilty of such lesser crime. The defendant has pleaded not guilty.

3.01 First-Degree Murder

Under the Criminal Code of the State of Nita a person commits the crime of first-degree murder if, after deliberation and with the intent to cause the death of a person other than himself, he causes the death of another person.

A person acts intentionally with respect to a result or to conduct described by a statute defining a crime when his conscious objective is to cause such result or to engage in such conduct.

Deliberation means that a decision to commit the act has been made after the exercise of reflection and judgment concerning the act.

To sustain the charge of first-degree murder the State must prove:

1. That the defendant performed the acts that caused the death of Donald Abbott; **and**
2. That the defendant acted after deliberation and with the intent to cause the death of Donald Abbott.

If you find from your consideration of all the evidence that each of these propositions has been proved beyond a reasonable doubt, then you should find the defendant guilty of first-degree murder.

If, on the other hand, you find from your consideration of all the evidence that any of these propositions has not been proved beyond a reasonable doubt, then you should find the defendant not guilty of first-degree murder.

3.02 Second-Degree Murder

Under the Criminal Code of the State of Nita, a person commits the crime of second-degree murder if:

1. He intentionally, but not after deliberation, causes the death of a person; **or**

2. With intent to cause serious injury to a person other than himself, he causes the death of that person or of another person.

A person acts intentionally with respect to a result or to conduct described by a statute defining a crime when his conscious objective is to cause such result or to engage in such conduct.

To sustain the charge of second-degree murder, the State must prove the following propositions:

1. That defendant performed the acts that caused the death of Donald Abbott; **and**

2. That defendant intended to kill or cause serious bodily injury to Donald Abbott.

If you find from your consideration of all the evidence that each of these propositions has been proven beyond a reasonable doubt, then you should find the defendant guilty of second-degree murder.

If, on the other hand, you find from your consideration of all the evidence that any of these propositions has not been proved beyond a reasonable doubt, then you should find the defendant not guilty of second-degree murder.

3.03 Manslaughter

Under the Criminal Code of the State of Nita, a person commits the crime of manslaughter if:

1. He recklessly causes the death of a person. A person acts recklessly when he consciously disregards a substantial and unjustifiable risk that a result will occur or that a circumstance exists; **or**

2. He kills another person while committing a misdemeanor inherently dangerous to other people; **or**

3. He intentionally, but not after deliberation, causes the death of a person, under circumstances where the act causing the death was performed upon a sudden heat of passion caused by a serious and highly provoking act of the intended victim, affecting the person killing sufficiently to excite an irresistible passion in a reasonable person. However, if between the provocation and the killing there is an interval sufficient for the voice of reason and humanity to be heard, the killing is murder.

To sustain the charge of manslaughter the State must prove the following propositions:

1. That defendant performed the acts that caused the death of Donald Abbott; **and**

2. That defendant acted recklessly; **or**

3. That the killing occurred while the defendant was committing a misdemeanor inherently dangerous to another person; **or**

4. That defendant intentionally caused the death of another under circumstances where the act causing death was performed upon a sudden heat of passion caused by a serious and highly provoking act of the intended victim.

If you find from your consideration of all the evidence that these propositions have been proved beyond a reasonable doubt, then you should find the defendant guilty of manslaughter.

If, on the other hand, you find from your consideration of all the evidence that either of these propositions has not been proved beyond a reasonable doubt, then you should find the defendant not guilty of manslaughter.

3.04 Negligent Homicide

Under the Criminal Code of the State of Nita, a person commits the crime of criminally negligent homicide if:

1. By conduct amounting to criminal negligence he causes the death of a person; **or**

2. He intentionally causes the death of a person, but he believes in good faith that circumstances exist that would justify his conduct, but his belief that such circumstances exist is unreasonable.

Conduct means an act or omission and its accompanying state of mind, or a series of acts or omissions.

A person acts with criminal negligence when, through a gross deviation from the standard of care that a reasonable person would exercise, he fails to perceive a substantial and unjustifiable risk that a result will occur or that a circumstance exists.

To sustain the charge of criminally negligent homicide, the State must prove the following propositions:

1. That defendant performed the acts that caused the death of Donald Abbott, a human being; and

2. That defendant acted with criminal negligence; or he acted intentionally, but believed in good faith that circumstances existed that would have justified the killing of Donald Abbott, and defendant's belief that such circumstances existed was unreasonable.

If you find from your consideration of all the evidence that each of these propositions has been proved beyond a reasonable doubt then you should find the defendant guilty of criminally negligent homicide.

If, on the other hand, you find from your consideration of all the evidence that either of these propositions has not been proved beyond a reasonable doubt, then you should find the defendant not guilty of criminally negligent homicide.

3.10 Self-Defense

The killing of another person in self-defense is justifiable and not unlawful when the person who does the killing actually and reasonably believes:

1. That there is imminent danger that the other person will either kill him or cause him great bodily injury; and

2. That it was necessary under the circumstances for him to use in self-defense such force or means as might cause the death of the other person, for the purpose of avoiding death or great bodily injury to himself.

A bare fear of death or great bodily injury is not sufficient to justify a homicide. To justify taking the life of another in self-defense, the circumstances must be such as to excite the fears of a reasonable person placed in a similar position, and the party killing must act under the influence of such fears alone. The danger must be apparent, present, immediate, and instantly dealt with, or so must appear at the time to the slayer as a reasonable person, and the killing must be done under a well-founded belief that it is necessary to save one's self from death or great bodily harm.

If the evidence of self-defense raises a reasonable doubt of the defendant's guilt, then you should find him not guilty of any criminal offense.

4.00 Concluding Instruction

You shall now retire and select one of your number to act as presiding juror. He or she will preside over your deliberations. In order to reach a verdict all jurors must agree to the decision. As soon as all of you have agreed upon a verdict, so that each may state truthfully that the verdict expresses his or her vote, have it dated and signed by your presiding juror and return with it to the courtroom.

IN THE DISTRICT COURT
OF THE STATE OF NITA
COUNTY OF DARROW

THE STATE OF NITA	)	
	)	Case No. 55827
vs.	)	JURY VERDICT
WALTER COLE,	)	
Defendant.	)	

We, the jury, return the following verdict, and each of us concurs in this verdict:

[Choose the appropriate verdict]

I. NOT GUILTY

We, the Jury, find the defendant, Walter Cole, NOT GUILTY.

_____   _____
Date   Presiding Juror

II. GUILTY

We, the Jury, find the defendant, Walter Cole, GUILTY of the crime of:

Murder in the First Degree

Murder in the Second Degree

Manslaughter

Criminally Negligent Homicide

_____   _____
Date   Presiding Juror

ॐ

The NITA Foundation

supports NITA's core values of excellence, ethics, mentoring, inclusiveness, justice, and philanthropy through our various programs. We strive to give back to our global community by supporting the work of attorneys engaged in the representation of the underserved, indigent, and disenfranchised. To learn more about NITA's publications, programs, or the work of our Foundation, please visit us online at www.nitafoundation.org or by calling (877) 648-2632.

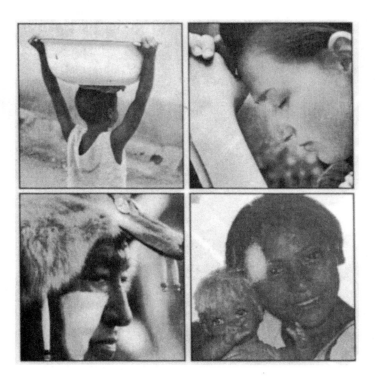

The NITA Foundation